MARY
QUEEN *of* SCOTS

As one of the most enduringly intriguing figures in history Mary Queen of Scots has fascinated historians and biographers for generations. She has inspired works in many languages by poets, musicians, writers and playwrights. She is portrayed as a romantic and tragic heroine, as a martyr, as an adulteress and murderess, and always controversial. The century she lived in saw the Reformation in Europe and a constant struggle for power among the kingdoms of England, France and Spain. Scotland's geographical location placed Mary at the centre of it all, in times when marriage was a political instrument. The key to her eventful life was her situation as a Scottish Queen who also had a claim to the English throne through intermarriage between both Royal Houses.

THE BEGINNING

The English House of Tudor began in 1485, when Henry Tudor of Lancaster defeated the reigning monarch Richard III at the Battle of Bosworth which ended the Wars of the Roses for the English Crown. Henry had himself crowned Henry VII and lost no time in marrying Elizabeth of York, uniting the two families.

In Scotland the Stewart dynasty had begun a hundred years earlier when Margery, daughter of Robert the Bruce, married Walter Fitzalan, whose family were Hereditary Stewards to the Kings of Scotland. He was known as Walter the Steward or simply Walter Steward. The surname became Stewart and later took the French form Stuart. From this union came the long line of Stuart Kings. One of these, James IV, married Margaret Tudor, daughter of Henry VII, making the link between the kingdoms.

For nearly three centuries from the end of the 13th to the late 16th there were few periods when Scotland enjoyed a long and peaceful reign. Kings succeeded to the throne as minors, some even as infants. The country had to be administered by Regents or Governors and this led to fierce rivalry among the great families for the power this office would bring.

King Robert I of Scotland – 'The Bruce'

Since the 11th century there had been disputes over the Border country stretching from the Central Lowlands in Scotland to Cumbria and Northumberland in England. Both sides raided the rich farmlands of the area, stealing cattle and pillaging towns and villages. In 1291 Edward I of England claimed feudal superiority over Scotland and the Wars of Independence followed, when William Wallace and Robert the Bruce emerged as national heroes, celebrated to this day.

In 1328 England finally recognised Scotland as an independent country

COURT, CHURCH AND COMMONS

The degeneration and corruption in the Church were satirised by the poet Sir David Lyndsey in Scotland's only morality play, 'Ane Satyre of the Three Estaits', first performed in 1540. Over four hundred years later it was one of the great successes of the Edinburgh International Festival.

with Robert the Bruce as king. During this time England was at war with France and many Scots fought on the French side, making a bond which would influence future events.

By the early 16th century the authority of the Roman Catholic Church was being challenged throughout Europe. Religious institutions had deteriorated spiritually and morally. Corruption was widespread and the church in Scotland was no exception. A strong Protestant movement started and attracted many sincerely religious people looking for guidance. James V did not oppose the Reformers. In England Henry VIII had already broken with Rome, seizing Church lands and redistributing them among his nobles.

The English Succession

Henry's ambition was to establish sovereignty over Scotland. He proposed

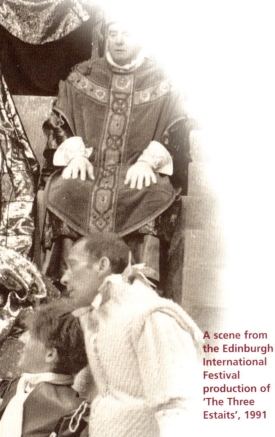

A scene from the Edinburgh International Festival production of 'The Three Estaits', 1991

MARY OF GUISE, JAMES V's QUEEN

The Guise family was one of the most influential in France, excelling in statesmanship and close to the King. Henry VIII had proposed marriage to Mary, but she had wisely declined. She had a surviving son from her first marriage, the seven-year-old Francis, whom she left in the care of his Guise uncles. She saw him only once more, and he was to die young.

a marriage between his daughter Mary Tudor and James, but James instead married the French King's daughter Madeleine. She died shortly after arriving in Scotland. James then married Mary of Guise, from a powerful French family, who had been widowed about the same time. She was known for her intelligence, courage and tolerance.

BIRTH *of a* LASS

Having failed to gain a hold on Scotland by marriage Henry resorted to force. In 1542 he invaded the country and in November the Scots army was defeated at Solway Moss, just over the border, with heavy losses and many of the Scots nobility captured. James was shattered. He visited his wife at Linlithgow (pictured above), where she was awaiting the birth of an heir. She had already borne two sons to James and both had died in infancy. After a few days James, still deeply depressed, retreated to his favourite hunting lodge, Falkland Palace. Here he was brought the news that the child was a daughter. He is reported to have said 'It cam' wi' a lass, it'll gang wi' a lass.' Six days later he died and the Crown passed to the infant Mary.

This tendency to physical collapse under stress ran in the Stuart family and later appeared in Mary herself. James was right in his prediction about the end of the dynasty, but 'the lass' it would pass with was not his daughter Mary.

The baby was said to be frail, but by the time she was two or three she was a lively little girl. She spent her first months at Linlithgow and was baptised in St Michael's Church there. An urgent matter was the appointment of a Regent. The times were troubled, the Reformation had taken hold in Scotland and the English were still hostile. In addition, though far in the future, there was the question of her marriage. In the end the 2nd Earl of Arran was appointed Regent. Though weak and indecisive he had a hereditary right to the post, which he held till supplanted by the Dowager Queen.

Henry VIII returned to his original project of uniting the kingdoms by marriage. He proposed that the infant Queen should be betrothed to his five-year-old son Edward. He gained support for this scheme among the Scots nobles he had taken prisoner at Solway Moss, by rewarding them with English pensions and allowing them to return to Scotland.

In July 1543 the Greenwich Treaties relating to the marriage were drawn up. The main point of contention was Mary's immediate future. In addition to the usual conditions of such a contract Henry wanted her brought up at the English Court under his supervision. The Scots insisted she stay in Scotland till she was ten years old.

Mary's cradle

Jedburgh Abbey, sacked during the Rough Wooing

By December the Scots had repudiated the agreement and Henry again tried force. Over the next two years he launched a brutal campaign which became known as the Rough Wooing. The Border abbeys were destroyed, burial grounds desecrated, harvests burned and villages and market towns razed. Edinburgh was attacked and Holyrood Palace badly damaged, though the Castle held out.

The Queen's Safety

There was a very real fear that the baby Queen might be seized and carried off. She was taken to Stirling and crowned there when she was nine months old. Even Stirling Castle was not thought secure enough and Mary was moved to the less accessible countryside. She spent some time at the Augustinian Priory on the island of Inchmahome in the Lake of Menteith, a peaceful and secluded place. The Prior there became her tutor and remained with her during her early years. Eventually she was taken to Dumbarton Castle in the west.

Meanwhile there was a new development in the already complex situation. In January 1544 the French Dauphiness gave birth to a son, a future heir

to the throne, presenting the possibility of an acceptable match for Mary. After some discussion and negotiation the Regent and Parliament agreed to Mary's betrothal to the baby prince, who had meantime become Dauphin on the accession of his father as Henry II of France. In July 1548 a fleet of French ships arrived at Dumbarton to take the little Queen to safety in France. She was not yet six years old.

The bond between Mary and her mother was a strong one. Throughout their lives they kept up a prolific correspondence and Mary set great store by her mother's counsel. They were only to see each other once more, when the Dowager Queen paid a visit to the French Court in 1550.

A STRATEGIC FORTRESS

Dumbarton Castle (above) stands on the banks of the Clyde near its estuary. It is virtually impregnable, protected by a huge rocky promontary on the landward side. It commanded the safer western sea route through the Irish and English Channels to France.

The HAPPY YEARS

Mary was accompanied by a retinue which included a number of children of her own age, sons and daughters of the Scots nobility. Her closest companions were four girls, the Four Maries.

Friends for life

From Dumbarton the flotilla sailed down the west coast and into the English Channel reaching France about a week later. The weather was very stormy but the little Queen seems to have been unaffected and even made fun of her seasick friends.

She had grown into a healthy, merry girl with great charm. She delighted everyone at Court and her Guise grandmother Antoinette took her to her heart from the first. This lady had the responsibility of settling her in her new surroundings, and thanks to her, Mary's years in France were to be the only secure and happy time in her life.

From the first the betrothed children were very fond of each other. Francis was a year younger than Mary, a delicate boy in contrast to her exuberance, possibly the attraction of opposites. At Court Mary acquired all the skills expected of ladies of her

THE FOUR MARIES

The name 'Marie' simply meant a lady-in-waiting. Mary Fleming was the daughter of her governess and a distant cousin of Mary herself. Mary Livingston was a daughter of Lord Livingston of Callander, a family with a long and close association with the Stuarts. Mary Beaton and Mary Seton had French mothers who had been ladies-in-waiting to Mary of Guise and had married Scots nobles.

A clarsach that is said to have belonged to Mary. The clarsach is a medieval Gaelic harp

A view of the palace and gardens at Fontainebleau, one of the palaces at which Mary stayed while at the French Court

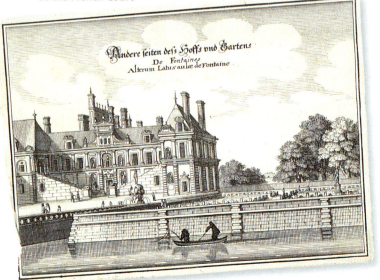

rank. She was taught Latin, Italian and
Spanish, with some Greek. She became
fluent in French, and although she never
forgot her Scots tongue, French was the
language she spoke and wrote in all her
life. She was an excellent dancer, sang
well and played the lute and other
instruments. She learned to draw
and was an accomplished
needlewoman, a skill which gave her
great pleasure through all her
troubles. Examples of her embroidery
have survived. In addition she received
instruction in statecraft from her Guise
uncles.

Marriage

The betrothal took place in April 1558
and was celebrated with elaborate
festivities. There were several days of balls,
banquets and spectacles and gifts were
distributed among the people. Though
there is doubt that the marriage was ever
consummated, Mary and Francis were obviously
devoted to each other, as all remarked.

In Scotland Mary of Guise had become Regent in
1554. She had appointed many French officials, and
this was resented. The religious conflict was now
very bitter. John Knox was the dominant figure. He
was a small man with a flowing beard and
penetrating eyes, an eloquent and fiery preacher. His
oratory often produced a violent reaction from his
followers.

**John Knox's House on the
Royal Mile in Edinburgh**

THE FOUNDING OF THE REFORMED
CHURCH

*Knox had been ordained a priest, but after a long struggle
with his conscience he left the Church. He first appeared as a
Reformer in 1546, when he was arrested by the Dowager
Queen's French troops and sent to the galleys. On his release he
went to England and then to the Continent, where he met
Calvin and other leaders of the Reformation. He returned to
Scotland confirmed in his hatred of Popery, determined to
work for a Reformed Church and intolerant of compromise.*

JOHN KNOX.

RETURN *to her* PEOPLE

Edinburgh Castle, a fortress from early times. Mary of Guise died here in 1560 and Queen Mary gave birth to the future James VI here in 1566

The Queen Regent had been supportive of the reforms, believing them best for Scotland. Now the behaviour of the mobs worsened, attacking and destroying churches and monasteries, tearing down statues and images and desecrating sacred vessels and vestments. The Dowager Queen could not tolerate this devastation. She responded by sending troops to stop the attacks. Some of the soldiers were French, causing further resentment.

The Reformers appealed to England for help, and when it arrived Leith, the port of Edinburgh, was besieged by Scots and English forces. During the conflict the Queen Regent moved to the Castle in Edinburgh for security and so that she could oversee the siege. She had contracted dropsy and was now seriously ill. Her condition deteriorated and by the spring of 1560 she was in great pain. Knowing she was dying she called together the leaders of the new Church. It was important to her that they should know she had always acted to protect and further the interests of Scotland as she saw them. It must

Wooden plaque depicting either Mary of Guise or Mary Tudor. This is one of a collection known as The Stirling Heads which decorated the ceiling of the King's apartment in Stirling Castle

Coin struck to commemorate the marriage of Mary to Francis, the French dauphin

have taken a tremendous effort, physically and mentally, but it was typical of her that even at the last she tried to fulfil her obligations. She had been an able Regent, fair and tolerant until revolted by the violence. Her life was full of tragedy, twice widowed, suffering the loss of infants and parting from two dear children. Her courage remained to the end. She died only a few days before her army was defeated and the siege ended.

The Treaty of Edinburgh in July followed and provided among other conditions that English and French troops should leave the country and that a new national Church should be established. The Parliament met and passed legislation rejecting the authority of the Pope, forbidding the celebration of the Mass and condemning all doctrines and beliefs except those drawn up by the Protestant ministers. There were heavy sanctions for those who broke these laws, including the confiscation of property, banishment and even death. The leaders also provided that there should be a school in every parish and higher schools in large towns, open to all. Unfortunately, the lands and possessions of the former churches had been seized by the nobles and there was no money to carry out these good intentions at the time.

In 1559 the young Queen's father-in-law Henry II died in a jousting accident and Francis succeeded to the French throne. In December the delicate Francis succumbed to an ear infection and died. Mary was just 18.

The choices begin

By the terms of her marriage contract Mary had the choice, if widowed, of remaining in France or returning to Scotland. She now had estates in France which would have allowed her to live very comfortably in a country she knew and loved. Considering this and the security her Guise family connections would have given her, she made a courageous decision to come back to the land where she believed her duty lay.

Mary chose as her advisers her half-brother James Stewart, an illegitimate son of James V, and William Maitland of Lethington who had been one of her mother's trusted councillors. They were both supporters of Protestantism and this choice was a further reassurance to the Reformers. She never sought to reinstate the former church and like her mother accepted the new order from the first, believing it was best for the country. She was ready to endorse it provided she and her household could continue to practise their own religion in private. She wanted above all to be accepted by her people.

In preparation for the journey to Scotland Mary asked Elizabeth of England for a passport to ensure a safe journey across the North Sea. England had control of the seas around her coasts and the permit would protect Mary if her fleet should be intercepted by English ships. Mary had not yet ratified the Treaty of Edinburgh, as her advisers thought she should wait till she consulted her Council when she got to Scotland.

Elizabeth was anxious that the religious reform in Scotland should be confirmed, and refused Mary's request when she heard the Treaty had not been ratified. Mary took the refusal with good grace. She wrote to Elizabeth in friendly terms, again asking for an assurance of safe conduct, but did not delay her departure. Elizabeth eventually did grant the passport but it arrived several days after Mary reached Scotland. It typified Elizabeth's ambivalent treatment of Mary.

Mary travelled round France, visiting all her French relatives to take her leave. She sailed from Calais in August, and the voyage was uneventful. Her convoy did encounter some English ships but no attempt was made to intercept the Queen's ships. Some of the other vessels in the convoy were stopped but finally allowed to continue on their way.

Mary disembarking at Leith. The young Queen received a warm welcome from her subjects on her way to Holyrood Palace

They reached Leith in four or five days, and on 19 August 1561 Mary stepped ashore onto Scottish soil. She had been away thirteen years.

One of those who had charge of planning the voyage was the Hereditary Lord High Admiral of Scotland, James Hepburn, Earl of Bothwell. He had received financial help from Mary some years earlier, at the French Court. In appearance he was of medium height and swarthy, with a strong physique and a compelling personality. He also had great charm.

Mary had a warm welcome from her subjects. With the establishment of the Reformed Church the religious climate was calm for a time. Once they were assured there would be no interference with their worship her people were ready to accept her.

She proceeded to Holyrood Palace, now repaired after the damage caused in the Rough Wooing. Her subjects lined the streets, eager to see the Court and to greet their Queen. There were performances by townspeople acting out appropriate themes and the celebrations were enthusiastic. Mary's appearance and bearing and the finery of her courtiers fulfilled their highest expectations and they were ready to enjoy the festivities after the troubled times.

Bonfires were lit and Mary was serenaded in the Palace all night by a large band of musicians playing a variety of instruments and singing psalms. By all

Holyrood Palace, the official residence of the monarch in Scotland

accounts it may not have given as much pleasure as they intended, for what they lacked in skill they made up for in volume. Nevertheless the next morning Mary thanked them for the performance and assured them she had greatly enjoyed it.

This ability to relate to others was a striking characteristic. Unbiased reports describe her as mature and intelligent, modest and ready to listen to advice with wisdom and good judgement. Even John Knox conceded her charm and feared her subjects would be won over by it.

Mary's most striking feature was her height. She was 5'10" or 11" (1.7m), unusual in a woman even today. Her figure was graceful and her hair red-gold, almost the colour of her eyes. Her complexion glowed thanks to her fondness for outdoor pursuits. She enjoyed hunting and hawking, played golf and croquet and practised archery. She liked to play cards and chess, and her library contained books on subjects such as history, music and astronomy. She introduced many of the pastimes and entertainments of the French Court, and believed it her duty to present a Queenly image and uphold the dignity of the Crown, with elegant gowns and jewels.

In September Mary set out on a Royal progress to visit her domain and make herself known to her people. She went first to Linlithgow where she was born and then to Stirling and Perth. In Perth she suffered a sudden mysterious illness, bouts of which were to recur all her life. It was never

A cameo pendant which belonged to Mary

identified, and may have been brought on by tension, though in those times the suspicion of poison was never absent. She showed her characteristic resilience and next day continued on to Dundee and St Andrews. On another progress she visited the north east, calling at Aberdeen and Inverness.

Stirling Castle. Mary was crowned here as an infant

An oil painting of Mary in mourning for Henry II of France, attributed to Francois Clouet

The FATEFUL YEARS

A depiction of one of the several stormy confrontations Mary had with John Knox

to be a ruler, and that subjects had the right to rebel in such a case, in a treatise against 'The Monstrous Regiment (Rule) of Women'.

Conflict

The interview was heated on both sides. Mary took him to task for inciting her subjects against her and against her mother before her. He finally agreed to accept the situation provided she did not interfere in religious matters. Some time later he preached a particularly scurrilous sermon against dancing, which he regarded as an invention of the Devil. He described Mary as dancing with glee on hearing of the persecution of the Huguenots in France. Brought up in the French court, Mary saw dancing as an innocent pleasure, and again there was a total lack of understanding between them. Knox finally agreed that dancing was acceptable if modest. Mary made further attempts to establish some kind of rapport, but without success. In spite of himself, Knox was impressed with her. He recognised her charm, and feared it. He said later that she had 'a proud mind, a crafty wit and an indurate (hard) heart, against God and his Truth'.

Mary had two main aims. She wanted to establish stable government with the co-operation of her people, and to ensure Elizabeth's acknowledgement of her right to the English succession. One of her first acts was to confirm the existing form of worship, though reserving the right to practise her own religion in private. She gave some of the former church lands and properties to the new Church of Scotland.

The following Sunday John Knox preached an inflammatory sermon against the Mass, and Mary summoned him to Holyrood. He was totally convinced of the righteousness of his cause and completely incapable of compromise. He had also been outspoken about the role of women, maintaining that it went against nature for a woman

When rumours of Mary's possible marriage to the Catholic heir to the Spanish throne became known, Knox again reacted violently. He preached vehemently against it, though the plans were tentative. Mary responded vigorously. She sent for him and complained that this time he had gone too far. Unrepentant, he took the opportunity to lecture her on the evils of a Catholic marriage and actually reduced her to tears, probably of frustration. She dismissed him. He continued his exhortations, warning his congregations to defend their faith.

HUSBAND *for a* QUEEN

Even as Mary's husband Francis lay dying, conjecture had begun about her next marriage. England, France and Spain had an interest in the choice of bridegroom. There was no shortage of candidates of Royal blood and of lesser rank. During the mourning period the options were weighed up by all concerned.

The Royal aspirants included the Kings of Denmark and Sweden, Philip of Spain's heir Don Carlos, the Archduke Charles of Austria, and also Francis' younger brother Charles, now twelve years old and King of France. Even the former Regent Arran saw the possibility of bringing about a match with his own son which he had proposed when Mary was an infant.

Mary herself was inclined to favour Don Carlos. He was three years younger than her and had been sickly from birth. Perhaps he reminded her of Francis whom she had loved in spite of his frailty. The deliberations about the marriage took some time, which was just as well: Don Carlos began to display signs of mental

A portrait of Elizabeth I by Marcus Gheeraerts the Younger. Elizabeth suggested her own favourite, Robert Dudley, Earl of Leicester, as a suitable husband for Mary

disorder and these became so undeniable that discussions were abandoned.

The consequences of marrying a Catholic had to be considered, even apart from John Knox's opposition. It could call into question her support of the Reformed Church, and might affect Elizabeth's recognition of Mary's claim to the English Crown. Elizabeth now let it be known that she would not countenance a foreign husband for Mary and hinted that she had a suitable bridegroom in mind.

He was Lord Robert Dudley, a great favourite of Elizabeth who had created him Earl of Leicester. There had been rumours that he might become her Consort. There was a great scandal when his wife was found dead, apparently having fallen down a flight of stairs. Elizabeth must have realised that marriage was impossible. She suggested him as a husband for Mary, strengthening English influence in Scotland. Dudley was less enthusiastic as he still had hopes of marrying Elizabeth. Mary and her advisers rightly considered the proposal insulting and it was politely declined.

Another choice

By 1565 Mary had been a widow for four years and a marriage seemed no nearer. In the spring of the following year the Earl of Lennox returned to Scotland from England. He had supported Henry VIII during the Rough Wooing and had fled the country. As a Catholic, he was regarded with some suspicion in England, but Elizabeth now allowed him to leave. In the spring of the following year he was joined by his son, Henry Darnley.

Henry was three years younger than Mary. He was even taller than her, slim and handsome with an athletic figure, golden hair and an outward charm. He shared her enthusiasm for outdoor diversions and was well schooled in Court etiquette. But all his contemporaries agreed on his character. Brought up by a father who doted on him and a mother with high ambitions for him, he was shallow, vain, arrogant and totally self-absorbed, with a quick and vicious temper.

To Mary, after the years of loneliness it must have seemed predestined. Both were grandchildren of James IV and traced their descent from Henry VII. Such a match would strengthen their claim to the English throne. It is not surprising that she fell deeply in love with her dazzling cousin. She refused to listen to her advisers and did not even wait for the Papal dispensation necessary to allow cousins to marry. She heaped honours on him, and a few days before the wedding had him proclaimed King, causing great resentment.

The ceremony took place on Sunday, 29 July in the royal chapel at Holyrood, followed by banqueting, dancing and masques. There were notable absentees, including her advisers, James, now Earl of Moray, and Maitland. Moray had been suspicious of Darnley from the start, and he organised a short-lived rebellion which became known as the Chaseabout Raid. Mary spent the first months of her marriage riding about the country at the head of her army seeking an engagement with the rebels. It

A ROMANTIC MATCH

Henry Stewart, Lord Darnley, was the son of the Earl of Lennox. His mother Margaret was the daughter of James IV's widow, Margaret Tudor, by her second marriage, and she considered she had a strong claim to both thrones. She had long thought to strengthen it by marrying Henry to Mary, and had twice sent him to the French Court with greetings for Mary.

was futile on both sides and by October Moray gave up and left the country, returning later after making his peace with Mary.

Mary's new advisers included Lennox and Bothwell. The latter had come back from abroad at her request, to give her the strong support she felt she needed. Already Henry was beginning to show his true colours. He spent his time with like-minded cronies and was so lax in his kingly duties that an iron stamp was made of his signature so as not to delay matters of state while he was away hunting.

By December Henry was openly pursuing a life of debauchery with his worthless companions and Mary had come to her senses. She was now pregnant.

DARKENING CLOUDS

Mary's household contained many who had come with her from France and she spent her leisure in their company. It included David Rizzio, an Italian who became a great favourite, and this was resented by the Scots nobility, and by John Knox who suspected him of being a Papal spy.

On 9 March 1566, a Saturday evening, Mary was enjoying a small supper party in her apartments at Holyrood. The rooms were directly above Henry's, connected by a narrow internal staircase. By now Henry seldom joined the Queen and the company was surprised when he appeared from the top of the stairs. Mary greeted him and was making a place for him when a band of armed men burst into the room after him. They seized Rizzio, manhandling the Queen herself to get at him. Henry restrained her and Rizzio was dragged out through the Queen's suite to the main staircase. His body was found at the foot, stabbed more than 50 times. Henry, jealous of the secretary and encouraged by his companions, had concurred in a plot to get rid of him.

During the next few days Mary managed to convince her husband that they were both in danger, and they escaped and fled to Dunbar Castle where Bothwell was waiting. There they gathered an army and returned to Edinburgh. Her people, appalled at the brutal events and pleased at the prospect of an heir, turned out to support her enthusiastically.

Rizzio's murder in the Queen's supper room

THE QUEEN'S FAVOURITE

David Rizzio came to Scotland as a retainer of the Savoyard Ambassador. He stayed on at Mary's request, to join her musicians. He was short and dark and considered ugly, but he had a great ability to entertain the Queen. When her Secretary died she appointed him to the post.

For safety Mary now moved to Edinburgh Castle to await the birth, and made a will giving instructions for the distribution of her jewellery and possessions, should she or the baby or both die. By far the greatest number of gifts to one person were left to Henry, 26 in all. They included the ring he had given her on their marriage.

The baby was born on 19 June after a long and difficult labour, a healthy boy. There was great rejoicing throughout the land and a thanksgiving service was held in St Giles Cathedral in Edinburgh. The baby was taken to Stirling Castle when he was a few months old, as his mother had been, and baptised there according to the Catholic rite in December. Queen Elizabeth was one of the god-parents, by proxy. Henry did not attend the ceremony and soon after left for Glasgow.

IACOBVS
DEI CRATIA
REX SCOTOR
ÆTATIS SVÆ I

1583

James VI of Scotland,
from a portrait of 1583

Hermitage Castle, seat of Bothwell's family. Mary rode to visit him here from Jedburgh, returning the same day

After the birth Mary left Edinburgh for a spell of recuperation in the countryside, accompanied by Moray and Bothwell. Darnley joined the party from time to time. She began to resume her royal engagements, and was holding a Court of Justice at Jedburgh in the Borders when she heard that Bothwell had been wounded in a local skirmish. She and Moray visited him in Hermitage Castle, returning the same evening. Since the flight to Dunbar Mary had relied on him more and more.

Some days later she fell seriously ill, and at one point her life was despaired of. It seems to have been an attack of the chronic abdominal pain which plagued her, and may have been caused by a haemorrhaging stomach ulcer, possibly exacerbated by anxiety and stress. After some fairly brutal medical procedures she made a full recovery.

Mary's health deteriorated after the birth, and from then on she was to suffer very severe bouts of illness, and was apparently near death on several occasions. Considering the physically punishing events during the pregnancy and the mental turmoil she experienced, it was not surprising. She would never again enjoy the robust constitution she had once had.

Cutting the knot

Meanwhile the Lords of Council were seeking a solution to the problem of her husband. Divorce was considered but possible complications, not least the legitimacy of Prince James, ruled it out. In the end a plan was drawn up to murder the King, and those involved put their names to a pledge. Among the names were those of Moray and Bothwell.

At Glasgow Henry had been taken ill, possibly with smallpox, but perhaps with a more sinister disease. When Mary heard of it she rode to Glasgow and brought him back to Edinburgh, where he was housed at Kirk o' Field not far from the Palace. Mary visited him and helped to nurse him. On 9 February she spent the evening with him as usual, but one of her ladies reminded her that she had promised to attend a midnight masque at the wedding of another attendant, and she went back to Holyrood.

At two in the morning an explosion was heard all over the town, and the house at Kirk o' Field was reduced to rubble. The bodies of Henry and his valet were found in their night clothes some distance away. They had been strangled. It was thought they had been alerted and tried to flee but were caught by the conspirators.

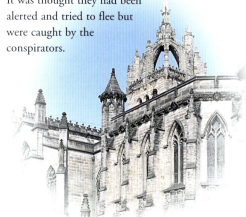

St Giles Cathedral, Edinburgh. A thanksgiving ceremony was held here following the birth of James VI

The BEGINNING of the END

JAMES HEPBURN, EARL OF BOTHWELL

Bothwell came from a boisterous but impecunious Border family who had always supported the Stuart kings. He had great personal courage and was well educated but erratic. He was thought rather rash and had already been involved in some dubious relationships.

Rumours of Bothwell's guilt were widespread and placards appeared accusing him of Darnley's murder. In response the Council mounted a trial, but Bothwell, himself now a Councillor, was acquitted.

After the murder Mary sank into a deep depression, like her father after Solway Moss. She herself was not excluded from suspicion and she was becoming increasingly isolated. She had always suffered unexplained bouts of sickness and abdominal pain. Now there was added the depression from which her father had suffered, and which affected her for the rest of her life. Perhaps it explains some of the extraordinary decisions she took.

Bothwell now aimed to become King by marrying Mary, and he had powerful support from the lords who believed he could restore stability. At the end of April he intercepted her returning with Maitland after a visit to her ten-month-old son at Stirling. It was the last time she saw the child. Bothwell

persuaded her to ride with him to Dunbar on the pretext that there was a disturbance in Edinburgh. There he ensured the success of his plan for marriage by ravishing the Queen. Again there are many questions about this, but it was confirmed by Maitland and shortly after by Mary herself.

In fact Bothwell already had a wife. He had married just a year before, with Mary's encouragement. Apparently it was a marriage of convenience, as his bride, Jean Gordon, paid off his debts. A divorce was now obtained with precipitate haste and Mary and Bothwell were married within a week. Mary was not allowed a Catholic Mass and there were no festivities.

The marriage lasted a month. Within days it was obvious that all was not well. Mary was frequently in tears and there were reports of quarrels and even suicide threats. The lords who had encouraged Bothwell now turned against him with the aim of liberating Mary, protecting the baby Prince and avenging Darnley, and gathered an army.

Bothwell and Mary set off for the Borders to muster support from among his people. Their pursuers caught up with them at Borthwick Castle, where Bothwell slipped away. Mary managed to make her escape dressed in men's clothing and the couple rode to Dunbar. Here they gathered troops and rode out

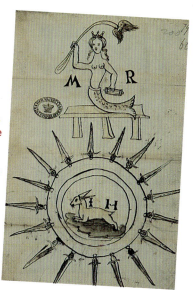

A placard displayed in the streets of Edinburgh following Darnley's murder. Mary is portrayed as a mermaid, the contemporary symbol for a prostitute. The hare was the Bothwell family crest

Loch Leven. Mary was imprisoned on the island in the middle of this loch

to meet the opposition, who were now calling themselves the Confederate Lords.

The two sides met at Carberry Hill not far from Edinburgh on 15 June. The Royal troops carried banners with the Cross of St Andrew, Scotland's patron saint, and the Lion Rampant of the Queen. The Confederate flag depicted the murdered Darnley and the infant Prince crying out for vengeance.

No battle took place. Bothwell offered to settle the outcome by single combat but Mary forbade it. Negotiations went on all day, and in the heat Bothwell's less disciplined forces began to drift away. The Lords sent a message that if Mary would leave Bothwell they would promise to restore her to her

A map of the Old Town of Edinburgh showing the Royal Mile connecting the Castle with Holyrood Palace. The street pattern is little changed today

rightful position. Realising her situation was hopeless she attempted a compromise, asking that Parliament investigate the murder, in the hope that Bothwell would be found innocent.

The Lords agreed to this and Bothwell took leave of the Queen. Before he rode away he gave Mary the bond which had sealed Darnley's fate. It had been signed by many of the Confederate Lords. It was the last time they saw each other.

The Fall

Mary had arrived at Dunbar in men's clothing, and the only women's clothes at the Castle belonged to servants. She was now wearing a simple gown with a red petticoat, ill fitting because of her height. She was horrified to find that she was jeered and roughly handled by the soldiers as she entered the Lords' camp, and no attempt was made to protect her.

Worse was to come in Edinburgh. The streets were lined with crowds screaming abuse and insults. She was not taken to the Castle or Holyrood but instead held captive at the house of the Provost and closely guarded by common soldiers. The mob surrounded the house deriding her with taunts and gibes. There were reports of her appearing at the windows, pleading for help, bedraggled and hysterical.

Meantime the Lords had to decide what to do with her. There was no thought of the promise they had given at Carberry. They needed time to cover up their own involvement in Darnley's murder and to settle her future and that of the Prince. Some of them had also taken the opportunity of carrying off many of her jewels and possessions.

Mary signs the Instrument of Abdication, under protest

She was moved to the Palace and reunited with her household. Thinking that the worst was over, she was having supper with her ladies when she was suddenly ordered to get ready to leave. They rode through the night, not as she expected to Stirling, but to Lochleven Castle.

The Castle stands on the largest of several islands in the loch about a mile from the shore. At that time the water level was higher than it is today and the waves lapped the very walls, making it particularly unassailable. It was in the charge of Sir William Douglas, a half-brother of Moray, their mother, Lady Margaret, having been a mistress of James V before her marriage.

No preparations had been made to receive Mary. She was given a room empty of furniture, even the bed was makeshift. She had very few clothes with her and only two servants. For the next few weeks she was prostrate and deeply depressed. By now she knew she was pregnant and this added to her physical and mental anguish.

Elizabeth had heard of Mary's plight and was outraged at this treatment of a monarch, but offered no help. Instead she suggested, as her father had done, that the infant heir should be brought to the English Court, ostensibly to be cared for by his maternal grandmother, Lady Lennox.

This concentrated the minds of the Lords. A decision about Mary was urgently needed. They drew up a warrant for her detention on the grounds of her association with Bothwell, her husband's murderer, and her possible involvement. Their main aim was to get her to agree to a divorce but she would not hear of it because of her pregnancy.

In late July Mary miscarried with twins and in her weakened condition she bowed to pressure and signed the Instrument of Abdication, protesting that she did so under duress and did not consider herself bound by it. She gave up the Crown to James, appointed Moray as Regent and agreed to a Council to act in his name.

On 29 July 1567 the baby Prince, aged 13 months, was crowned James VI of Scotland at Stirling. It was exactly two years since Mary had married Darnley.

In the Castle at Lochleven her living conditions remained spartan for some time. The Douglases had little sympathy for her at first. Lady Margaret had hoped to marry James V herself and resented Mary of Guise and of course Mary herself, whom she thought occupied a throne that should have been her son Moray's. Mary's gift of relating to those around her gradually softened them and Sir William at least seems to have accorded her some respect. She was allowed to send for more clothes and personal belongings. Members of her household joined her, among them Mary Seton, who was skilled at dressing the Queen's hair, raising her morale further. Mary was able to take up some of the diversions she loved, embroidery, cards and even music, though she had no opportunities for outdoor activities.

By now the people's antagonism towards her had been replaced by anger at the appalling treatment she had received. Support for her was growing among her ordinary subjects and some of the nobles.

ESCAPE

Some of the younger members of Sir William's household became very fond of Mary. In particular she captivated his younger brother George and George's cousin Willie. She made one or two attempts to escape which were discovered, but at the beginning of May with the help of these two she finally managed to get away from her captors.

George had rallied support on the shore and Willie created a distraction within the castle during which he managed to steal the keys. Mary herself diverted attention by engaging in an altercation with Lady Margaret. Dressed in servant's clothes and accompanied by one of her ladies she was rowed across the loch under cover of darkness and joined her supporters on the shore.

They rode to Niddry Castle just outside Edinburgh where they were warmly greeted by the local people. Mary issued a proclamation asking her subjects to rally to her and they responded with enthusiasm.

The following day the Queen's party proceeded to Hamilton where they gathered a large army, including some of the former conspirators who now sought to gain control of the Queen. Once again she was a political pawn.

There were two courses open to her to regain the throne. She could ask Parliament to annul the abdication or she could fight the Regent Moray. Now that the tide seemed to have turned in her favour and she had strong support she chose to fight.

The last battle

Dumbarton Castle was held by forces loyal to the Queen, and the Regent's forces mounted a siege. The Queen set off to relieve it. Her forces were intercepted at Langside, a small hamlet a few miles south of Glasgow. Mary had by far the larger force,

perhaps twice as many as her opponents. In the event victory went to the Regent because of the superior tactics of his commanders and the ineptitude of Mary's. The Duke of Argyll had provided the largest contingent of the Royal army and so was made supreme General. At the decisive moment he failed to throw in troops in support of the advance guard and the battle was lost. The Queen's forces retreated and fled the field.

Mary now had no hope of reaching Dumbarton. She rode south towards Galloway which was still strongly Catholic, hoping for reinforcements. It was a gruelling three-day journey over 90 miles of rough country, depending for food on poor isolated cottages and sleeping on the bare ground. At Dumfries Mary took stock. She could hope to gather a strong enough army, or she could sail to France where she had lands and friends.

Inexplicably she made another disastrous decision. She chose to appeal to her cousin Elizabeth for support. She set off in a fishing smack across the Solway Firth, and stepped ashore on the Cumbrian coast on 16 May with a small entourage.

After Carberry Hill Bothwell tried to raise support for Mary. The Lords charged him with murdering Darnley, abducting the Queen and forcing marriage on her. He was outlawed with a price on his head and his lands confiscated. Evading capture he sailed to Scandinavia where he was arrested. He spent his last years in one prison after another, finally losing his mind. He died in Dragsholm Prison in Denmark, where his mummified remains can still be seen in a neighbouring church.

Fading hopes

Mary's arrival in England presented Elizabeth with a dilemma. Although incensed at Mary's treatment by the Lords she was well aware that Mary could became a central figure to English Catholics. If she refused her support, Mary might turn to France.

There was the difficulty of where she should be housed. The obvious place for a monarch, even deposed, was at Court, and Mary took this for granted. That too could threaten Elizabeth. She decided to keep Mary in the North, far away from Westminster. Her excuse was the still unresolved charge of Mary's involvement in her husband's murder and marriage to the man suspected of it. Once Mary's innocence was established all would be well.

Mary had come to England of her own accord to ask for help. Elizabeth now construed this as giving her a mandate to judge the issue. Mary at first indignantly denied this right, but when Elizabeth promised to restore her to her throne when the enquiry found in her favour, she gave in.

Elizabeth was in contact with the Regent Moray who still maintained Mary's guilt, and as proof sent copies of the Casket Letters. These were letters, allegedly from Mary to Bothwell, said to be love letters and poems written before the murder and therefore implicating her. They were contained, along with other personal papers, in a small silver casket which was handed over by Bothwell's tailor under torture.

Mary denied writing the letters, but was never allowed to see them and from the start there were doubts about their authenticity. The Commission appointed by Elizabeth, after long deliberation, finally came to the unsatisfactory conclusion that neither side had proved their case.

Hi mihi funt Comites quos ipsa pericula ducunt

In quo quis peccat
In eo punitur.

Babington with his Complices in St Giles fields.

Sir Anthony Babington's plot was the instrument of Mary's arrest and execution

The long years

The remaining years of Mary's life were spent in captivity. After the indecisive result Elizabeth's Councillors advised her that Mary must be given no opportunity to move against her in any way. There had been a tentative uprising by the Catholic nobility in the North of England with the object of placing Mary on the throne. Doomed from the start it came to nothing, but it provided justification for her detention and isolation from contact with the outside world.

The relationship between the Royal cousins had always been enigmatic on Elizabeth's side. Mary's feelings were eagerly cordial and her desire for a meeting was a strong and recurring theme. Elizabeth's motives are less clear. Although she kept Mary a prisoner, often in very poor conditions, she was reluctant to sanction some measures suggested by her advisers. Even at the end, she procrastinated in taking the ultimate step of authorising Mary's execution. She offered a pardon if Mary would confess, and it was said the authorisation for the execution was concealed among a batch of official papers for her signature, to spare her feelings.

As the years passed Mary's health continued to

deteriorate. She had always suffered bouts of depression and severe pain. Now she developed crippling arthritis. Her only contact with the outside world was through letters and she maintained a constant interchange with her connections in France and Spain. She became resigned to her plight, her resistance worn down by ill-health. Perhaps despair and physical debility explain her involvement in the Babington Plot.

Sir Anthony Babington belonged to a Catholic group who formed a plan to place Mary on the English throne. They intended to assassinate Elizabeth, and Mary was aware of this, and appeared to encourage them in letters. Like all such groups they had been infiltrated by agents of the Crown and the details of the plot were known to the authorities.

Some years before, the English Parliament had passed an Act of Association which made it treasonable for anyone with a claim to the throne to be connected with a plot against the Queen under pain of death. Mary was arrested in August 1586. She insisted on her innocence, but was taken to Fotheringhay Castle to await trial.

The END *of* HOPE

The trial began at Fotheringhay on 15 October. Mary protested that the court had no jurisdiction over her as she was not Elizabeth's subject, nor were the Commissioners her peers. She had to conduct her own defence and was not allowed to call witnesses. She finally agreed in order to deny that she personally had ever plotted against Elizabeth, but she knew that under the Act of Association she would be found guilty. She intended to leave a lasting record of her defence. It was the first time she had been seen in public since she arrived in England.

The proceedings lasted two days, during which Mary defended herself passionately in spite of her physical frailty. When all the evidence had been heard the Commissioners returned to Westminster to consider their verdict. On 25 October they pronounced Mary guilty, taking care to dissociate James from the charge.

The penalty was loss of any claim to the succession followed by death. They presented a petition to Elizabeth for Mary's execution. The Queen temporised, asking them to find an alternative to the death penalty.

Mary herself was not told of the sentence until the middle of November. She had spent the time in preparation and was resolved to present herself as a martyr to the cause of Catholicism.

Elizabeth postponed signing the death warrant till January. On 8th February the sentence was carried out at Fotheringhay.

Courage

Mary spent the night before making a will and wrapping her few remaining possessions as keepsakes for her household. At six in the morning she got up, took leave of her servants and handed them the packets. Just before nine she was escorted

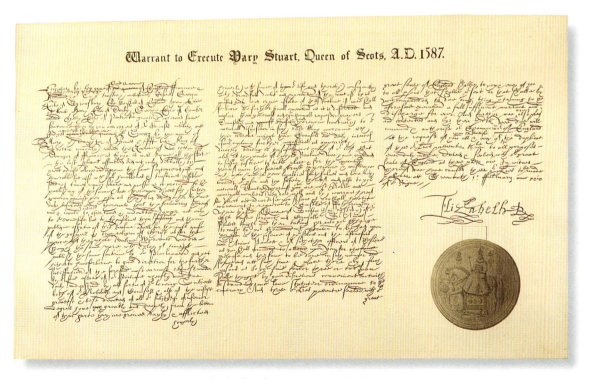

Mary's death warrant, signed by Elizabeth, after some prevarication

Mary's fan, one of the relics which now remain

to the main hall. A raised wooden stage had been erected, draped in black. On it was the execution block, also black-draped. She wore a black satin gown with a red petticoat and on her head a long white veil.

Two of her gentlewomen accompanied her to the block and helped to remove her outer garments. Her hair was bound up under the white veil which also covered her eyes. Mary continued praying as she laid her head on the block.

The executioner took two strokes to sever the head. Picking it up to display it to those present the white veil and the hair under it came away. It was a wig, and the head with Mary's own short grey hair fell to the ground. Some of those who saw it claimed that the lips were still moving. Grotesquely, when the clothes were removed from the body, one of Mary's little pet dogs was found whimpering among them.

All traces of the execution were obliterated for fear of fuelling a cult of relics. The body was kept at Fotheringhay for five months, before being interred in Peterborough Cathedral.

Mary had not seen her son since his infancy. She had done her best to maintain contact during her captivity, sending letters and gifts, but none reached him. He was

The scene of the execution of Mary Queen of Scots at Fotheringhay

schooled by a succession of Regents to hate his father and mother. His reaction to his mother's execution was equivocal. He was now first in line to the English succession, and though he broke off formal contact for a time, he soon accepted Elizabeth's justification for the deed.

In 1603 he finally succeeded to the English Crown on the death of the childless Queen, becoming James VI and I of the country which would be known as Britain. He commissioned a magnificent white marble tomb for his mother, and in 1612 Mary's remains were brought to lie in Westminster Abbey, near her cousin Elizabeth's.

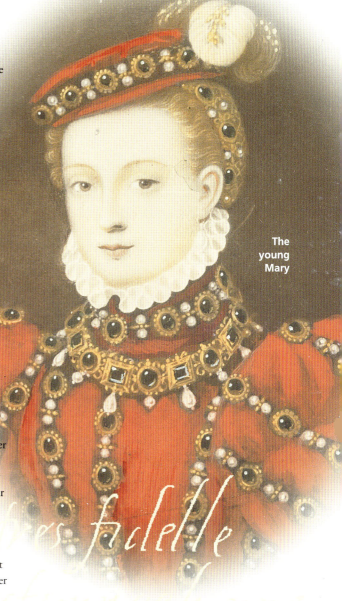

The young Mary

Aftermath

For the next few hundred years the centre of government and trade was in London. Ambitious and able Scots left their country to seek their fortunes abroad and today the Scottish diaspora is respected throughout the world.

A direct consequence of Mary's death was the attempted invasion of England by Philip II of Spain. He believed Mary had ceded to him her claim to the English throne if her son did not become a Catholic. Philip assembled the mighty Spanish Armada and launched his attack the year after Mary's execution.

In the late nineteenth century Mary's tomb was opened during a search for that of James. It was found to contain the coffins of many later Stuart descendants, among them that of James' daughter Elizabeth who became the Winter Queen of Bohemia. Her daughter Sophia married the Elector of Hanover. On the death of Queen Anne without issue in 1714, Sophia's son George became the first Hanoverian monarch of Britain. Elizabeth was the lass with whom the Stuart name passed, but Stuart blood has flowed in the veins of every British ruler since then.

The events of Mary's life, the enigma of her character and her bearing in her final days are enough to explain the spell she casts over so many. Truly, in her own words, in her end was her beginning.

Mary's effigy on her tomb in Westminster Abbey

MARIA
D   G
SCOTIÆ
PIISSIMA REGINA
FRANCIÆ DOTARIA
ANNO
ÆTATIS REGNIQ
36
ANGLICÆ CAPTIVIT
10
S   H
1578

Portrait of Mary
during her captivity